TREE OF STRINGS

Poets Published in
The Phoenix Living Poets Series

*

TREE OF STRINGS

By

NORMAN MacCAIG

CHATTO AND WINDUS

THE HOGARTH PRESS

1977

Published by
Chatto & Windus Ltd
with The Hogarth Press Ltd
42 William IV Street
London WC2N 4DF

*

Clarke, Irwin & Co. Ltd
Toronto

British Library Cataloguing in Publication Data
MacCaig, Norman
    Tree of strings. — (The Phoenix living poets).
ISBN 0-7011-2220-X
1. Title   2. Series
821'.9'12   PR6025.A1
    English poetry

Printed in Great Britain by
Redwood Burn Ltd
Trowbridge and Esher.

For A.K. MacLeod

CONTENTS

MORNINGS

What morning is this morning? Hidden in its rain
is the nameless morning I recognise.
(Even the sparrows are silent, a bedragglement
in a bigger one, and a car hisses
in a tree in drenched Eden.)

Yesterdays and tomorrows I can tell only
by the clothes they wear — by their scarves,
their raincoats or their Opening of Parliament
robes and blinding maces and croziers.
But it's no use to tell me
this morning is Thursday. I recognise only
the naked one under the clothes, whose scientific name
is *morning morning morning.* — I will die
of Thursdays and Fridays, but till then
this one will keep me alive, pensive acrobat
over timelessness, thoughtfully observing
the clock of sparrows, the calendar of cars passing,
the stopwatch of the sun.

STARS AND PLANETS

Trees are cages for them: water holds its breath
To balance them without smudging on its delicate meniscus.
Children watch them playing in their heavenly playground;
Men use them to lug ships across oceans, through firths.

They seem so twinkle-still, but they never cease
Inventing new spaces and huge explosions
And migrating in mathematical tribes over
The steppes of space at their outrageous ease.

It's hard to think that the earth is one —
This poor sad bearer of wars and disasters
Rolls-Roycing round the sun with its load of gangsters,
Attended only by the loveless moon.

IN EVERYTHING

Once I was on a cliff, on a ledge of seapinks,
Contemplating nothing — it was a self-sufficient day
With not a neurotic nerve to zigzag in the blue air.
Was that happiness? (Yes.) I sat, still as a shell,
Over water, in space, amongst spiders in chinks.

But suddenly I was introduced to suddenness.
As though a train entered a room, a headlong pigeon
Cometed past me, and space opened in strips
Between pinions and tail feathers of the eagle after it —
It had seen me. What vans of brakes! What voluptuousness!

What a space in space, carved like an eagle,
It left behind it! Below me the green sea-water
Wishy-washed, the blind thing, and the corally seapinks
Nodded over my hand. How can there be a revelation
In a world so full it couldn't be more full?

The pigeon hurtled out of my life. And I don't remember
The eagle going away. But I'll never forget
The eagle-shaped space it left, stamped on the air.
Absence or presence? . . . It seems I'm on a ledge of seapinks
All the time, an observing, blank-puzzled cliff-hanger.

THE DROWNED

Somebody said wrecks
come ashore, looking for the drowned
crews, as if they felt guilt, or love, or loneliness.

Timbers for boats, bones for men.

Their friends shut their minds, their
recollections, themselves
to the dogfish love, the ten inch wide
appetite of crabs.

. . . The tide washes in. And somebody
sings a song. And his friend, picked clean
to the delicate timber of bones,
drifts in the song, complete
as an archangel.

NOTHING TOO MUCH

He draws one line,
two, three, four, five,
not knowing what he's doing
except that he's sending feathery invitations
to Apollo.

He draws the fifteenth line
and Apollo yawns and stretches
and saunters in.

At the fortieth line
Apollo cries *Stop*!

Twenty lines later
Apollo's asleep in the rough web
of his certainties
and the artist is staring at
still another picture
he has choked to death.

Apollo stirs. He mutters
Artists! and sinks back
into the boring world
of perfection.

UNPOSTED BIRTHDAY CARD

I would like to give you
a thought like a precious stone
and precious stones a thought
couldn't think of.

When you see the lolling tongues
in the shadows, I would like to change them
to gentle candles whose grace
would reveal only yours.

I would like to place you
where the fact of the fairytale
and the fact of the syllogism
make one quiet room
with a fire burning.

I would like to give you
a whole succession of birthdays
that would add up only
to this one: that would be
without years.

MIDNIGHT ENCOUNTER

Of all the roses on the rose bush
the head of one lolled over the fence,
a fiery bucolic seraph
contemplating the weather
in heavenly turnip fields.

What must have been a man
came from the house and, saying nothing,
snipped off the rose
and gave it to me.

At home
I look at it and am not blinded,
I touch it and am not burned.

And I see what must have been a man
silently go back into his house
with a star by his side, a twinkle
of heavenly secateurs.

CONVICTED

On the day of the trouble
I knew nothing about it.

When it was all over and bulletins
clotted on the walls
I felt I'd been abandoned, I felt I'd been
exiled at home while others
marched off
into the wild land of suffering.

— The truth is I was locked
in the shameful prison of myself.
He struggled, she died in the foul air
where good and evil created
another evil, while there I sat
admiring
the shadows of the bars
on the floor of my cell.

SURVIVORS

The last wolf in Scotland
was killed two centuries ago.

I'd like to speak with it.
I wouldn't ask
why it opened the throats of deer and
tore mountain hares to pieces.
I wouldn't ask why it howled
in the corries and put one paw
delicately in a mountain torrent.

— It would have nothing to ask me
except, 'Why am I
the last wolf in Scotland?'

I would know what it meant,
for I am the last of my race
as you are, and she, and he.

We would look strangely at each other
before it loped back to its death
and I again put one foot
dangerously into the twentieth century.

FISHERMAN'S PUB

I leaned on the bar, not thinking, just noticing.
I read the labels thumbed on the bright bottles.
(To gallop on White Horse through Islay Mist!

To sail into Talisker on Windjammer Rum!)
Above my head the sick TV trembled
And by the dartboard a guitar was thrumming

Some out of place tune. . . Others have done this
Before me. Remember, in one of the Russias,
Alexander Blok drunk beyond his own mercy —

How he saw, through the smoke and the uproar,
His 'silken lady' come in and fire
The fire within him? I found myself staring

For mine, for that wild, miraculous presence
That would startle the world new with her unforgivingnes
But nothing was there but sidling smokewreaths

And through the babble all I heard was,
(Sounding, too near, in my dreadful silence)
A foreign guitar, the death clack of dominoes.

SPEAKING IN TUNE

I walk into a nowhere or a somewhere
and there you always are, my elegant cliché,
my witty recurring decimal.

When I was a boy and intrusive adults
asked me what I wanted to be when I grew up,
I used to say, 'A string quartet.'
That's when I didn't say,
'A retired bank manager.'

Now, in my splendid middle age,
I find, because of you,
I'm both.

Metaphorically, of course.
Just as, metaphorically,
you are my elegant, my witty
·9 repeater —
my dearest and nearest approximation
to the incomprehensible, powerful cliché
of zero, round which is gathered
the universe of all measures.

NOTATIONS OF TEN SUMMER MINUTES

A boy skips flat stones out to sea — each does fine
till a small wave meets it head on and swallows it.
The boy will do the same.

The schoolmaster stands looking out of the window
with one Latin eye and one Greek one.
A boat rounds the point in Gaelic.

Out of the shop comes a stream
of Omo, Weetabix, BiSoDol tablets and a man
with a pocket shaped like a whisky bottle.

Lord V. walks by with the village in his pocket.
Angus walks by
spending the village into the air.

A melodeon is wheezing a clear-throated jig
on the deck of the *Arcadia*. On the shore hills Pan
cocks a hairy ear; and falls asleep again.

The ten minutes are up, except they aren't.
I leave the village, except I don't.
The jig fades to silence, except it doesn't.

CLASS

A stone speaks. Don't tell me a stone
is inarticulate as a man.

It has no idea of class. Though it speaks fondly
of Baalbek and the Parthenon, it gossips, too, of
its glancing cousins in a mountain stream
and those smudged and fudged in roadside ditches.

If men, in their mist of words, their stumblings and
           torrents of words,
could say as much. How they would then praise
the pebbles on a beach, those bright rhetoricians.

COMPOSERS OF MUSIC

Musicians, calling in your circles and phases,
helpless in their ruminant fire,
unable to speak anything
but the laws of miracles,
how can you fail to shed
your tremulous humanity? How can you carry
your spongebag heart, your tick-tocking brain
along those orbits where you go
without skidding — without dying
into the clusters of notes you explode
in the earth's dark mind?

— I regard you with joy and with envy
from my thicket of words.

VENUS

Venus, that shrewd opposite,
scatters coins of cardboard
that buy kingdoms.

Then she smiles her buttonhook smile —
thinking of all those crowned heads glittering
in the smoke of insurrections;
thinking of the proud exiles gathered
in the sad cafés of the world.

The air was on the point of creaking. Every overhang
was fanged with icicles. No bird stirred
on the white mountains.

In my head was a glass of wine, a ruby,
a poppy head in the wilderness.

The snow squeaked under my feet, the cold
clasped my two wrists.

But in my head was something that excused me
to the weather. I apologised to the air
that spidered on my face.

I was warm with the place I was going to
and the woman in it. They made
the one glowing thing in a winter landscape.
I walked through it, balancing
my lantern head.

WAXWING

Waxwing, smart gentleman, gaudy bank manager
in your leafy bank, your swept-back crest
is the only thing about you that looks wind-blown.
Do you never face down-wind
or fly across the grain of a breeze?
Do you look with hauteur
when the grebe's crest frays sideways
and the lapwing's top-knot unravels?

I watch you choking down
plump, crimson berries – and the bank manager becomes
a lorry driver in a hurry
gobbling and gulping
in the wayside café of this branchy cotoneaster.

So many colours being busy at once!
Such a dandified gluttony!

You flirt to another branch:
and the wax-blob berry on your either side
winks among the clusters.

So a fold in a paper's a fold in a wave,
Universalist, monist, man out of love
With prevarications and discrepancies? That means
You and I are zero and not two ones.

But the essence! you shout, with the mad light
Of mysticism lotused in each eye. My foot
Gives its Johnsonian kick and the stone says,
I'm not a bird's flight, nor am I marshmallows.

You wriggle on your own pin. You scan
With affection yourself, your own specimen,
In a corner of the universal laboratory
Full of cancers and loves and ways of saying No.

Once upon a remarkable time Chaos
Stopped hiccuping, took a deep breath — and there was
A separation into separations:
Infinity exploded into infinite ones.

Do I prevaricate? Can I be an abstract budgie,
An essential chair, a universal snow
Since my right hand doesn't know what my left hand's doing
And if I'm wrong I'm right to be wrong?

Easier to believe (and as hard to give proof)
A thing isn't startlingly the same thing as itself.
So ho hum, philosopher, prove the opposite.
I assemble to hear you. I listen numerously.

INCALCULABLE YOU

Take four and a moment.
Four what? Four deaths,
four strangenesses of light, four
empires, four boats leaving harbour.

The size of a moment
that can handily hold
four galaxies! I think this, staring
at the four buttons
on your dress.

Had I been looking
at your eyes, it would have been
Take two and a moment —
my mistress of numerology,
my mysterious, my necessary
zero.

BESIDE A WATER

The night sat on the quay and I beside it,
Watching the slippery moon. The tide kept trying
To touch my feet. I thought *This is a proper night
For cicadas*. But Scottish grasshoppers were fast asleep.
That fitted the reconciliations that made the sky
Talk so lovingly, so gently to the deep mountain.

Someone, Medea, was crying in a Greek theatre
Shaped like a corrie. My hand clenched on the brooch
That was to blind Oedipus. Cuchulain, forgetting
His confounded nobility, scratched the side of his nose. . .
It was nice to think of the lobsters down there in the ebb
Swimming backwards through the tangle, being orchidaceous.

(There are faults even in a fault. That comforts me. My sore
                                                   lip
May prove I'm handsome. My first class honours degree
In stupidity may mean I'm a sage. Is it too much to hope
I have a silence in me that never heard
Of words?) . . . I noticed I was trying not to notice
A nudging seapink. I greeted it, across my border.

A moon-glance went by like Catullus on Loch Roe's
Hendecasyllabics. There was a Lesbia somewhere — as if
I needed to be told that. Mine was being orchidaceous
In her swimmingly way. . . Claws and all, I wretchedly
                                                   thought:
And concentrated on a ripple trying to turn a corner
On one foot, like Charlie Chaplin. It couldn't do it.

NOTES ON A WINTER JOURNEY, AND A FOOTNOTE

1

The snow's almost faultless. It bounces back
the sun's light but can do nothing with
those two stags, their cold noses, their yellow teeth.

2

On the loch's eye a cataract is forming.
Fistfuls of white make the telephone wires
mile after mile of snow buntings.

3

So few cars, they leave the snow snow.
I think of the horrible marzipan
in the streets of Edinburgh.

4

The hotel at Ullapool, that should be a bang of light,
is crepuscular. The bar is fireflied
with whisky glasses.

5

At Inchnadamph snow is falling. The windscreen wipers
squeak and I stare through
a segment of a circle. What more do I ever do? . . .

6

(Seventeen miles to go. I didn't know it, but when
I got there a death waited for me — that segment
shut its fan; and a blinding winter closed in.)

A. K. MACLEOD

I went to the landscape I love best
and the man who was its meaning and added to it
met me at Ullapool.

The beautiful landscape was under snow
and was beautiful in a new way.

Next morning, the man who had greeted me
with the pleasure of pleasure
vomited blood
and died.

Crofters and fishermen and womenfolk, unable
to say any more, said,
'It's a grand day, it's a beautiful day.'

And I thought, 'Yes, it is.'
And I thought of him lying there,
the dead centre of it all.

FINALITY

I have a longing to go
to a place that isn't here.
I'll go there soon.

I have a longing to meet
a man who isn't there.
I'll never see him again.

The places of the world
can be visited
and the people in them.

But he's in a nowhere
without journeys, without places,
without him.

Two harpsichords playing —
and there's a robust heaven:
no lackadaisical boredom of the infinite here,
no epicene angels being languid,
not a golden pavement in sight.
The logic of passion, made articulate,
invents fibres in the listening mind
that shape it from shapelessness.
A marriage is happening
in the holy precinct of reason — a consecration
of the elements of being — each
in its own distinction. They make it possible
to believe in the original Word that changed
being to becoming.

Cupola, half shell of white air,
vault of the idea of snowdrops,
white balance of forces,
you are the proper pureness to contain
this revelation of the ordinary
where the coloured windows let in
no light that's intrusive
and the corrupt mind is healed, for a time,
of its corruption —
in a shadowless place,
a place of benign voltages.

If a thing exists. . . How I hate sentences,
Mr. Professor, that begin with *if*.
Tilt your nose, Mr. Professor, and sniff

The vinegar of existence with a wild rose growing in it,
Hear the ravishing harmony dunted with a drum thud.
Put a hand on your throat — that beating is blood,

Not a pussyfooting echo of remote subjunctives.
The name of a thing means one thing and
The thing means another: fanfare for the ampersand

That joins and separates them with a third meaning.
Good ampersand: bad murderous if.
Tilt your nose, Mr. Professor: there's a whiff

Of heretical impatience in your fantasies
That won't let the world be. Are you so wise
You can add one more to the world's impossibles?

DECEPTIONS

Swimming slowly in line,
head, humped back, head, humped back —
two otters. Or one monster?

I watched them, rod held high, three flies
streaming in the wind. I watched them
from another time, from another place.
Might it be that the monster I'd seen there
was as innocent as the two otters
loitering through the ripples on Loch Lexie?

A fox barked on the hill. When I looked round again
the water was flat and unbroken as if
no otters existed in the whole world.

BUS STOP

No bus, no bus. . . As though I'm a field
I'm cropped by boredoms, black bulls the lot of them. . .
My mind does a Houdini with time and space:
I'm casting a fly over far Loch Cama.

Behind me the cut-price shop says *Whisky*
From £3.59. I look in my cut-price
Mind, but what's for sale there? — old junk,
Cobwebbed and cranky, with parts missing.

I tread on a glowing fag-end, with such
Satisfaction I wonder what else I'm treading on
And don't want to know. . . I'm pulling a boat
That's not there up on grouchy shingle.

That girl's handbag's an untidy temple
Of icons, incense and cruel rituals.
Sweet priestess, sacrifice me. . . A newsboy
Gouts from his split face tortured vocables.

And I lift a wineglass — I'm a 1930's actor
Tête-à-têting in a naughty nightclub,
And oh, seductively, leeringly, smile
At a 14 bus, at a taken-aback driver.

ANCESTRY

The ghost I never saw
and don't believe in
won't go away.

He speaks to me
but won't answer me.
When I whirl round
he's never there.

Should I be rural
and put out food for him?
— I'm not Homeric enough
to leave on the table
a bowl of blood.
And there's no need for that —
he drinks mine. . .

. . . Why should I feel the taste of it
in my own mouth?

WHAT DO YOU THINK?

Does bog asphodel
live up to its name?
Or liverfluke to its?
One of the periwinkles does
and one of the cataracts does.
But what about puce?
What about Peebles?

You must put names
to all my meanings.
Are they as true to me
as periwinkle to its shell
or do you name them so largely
my true self comes to you
as dwarfish, mean and ridiculous?

GRANDCHILD

She stumbles upon every day
as though it were a four-leaf clover
ringed in a horseshoe.

The light is her luck — and its thickening
into chair, postman, poodle
with a ribbon round its neck.

She plays among godsends
and becomes one. Watch her being
a seal or a sleepy book.

Yet sometimes she wakes in the night
terrified, staring
at somewhere else.

She's learning that ancestors
refuse to be dead. Their resurrection
is her terror.

We soothe the little godsend
back to us
and pray, despairingly —

May the clover be
a true prophet. May her light be
without history.

STONECHAT ON CUL BEG

A flint-on-flint ticking — and there he is,
Trim and dandy — in square miles of bracken
And bogs and boulders a tiny work of art,
Bright as an illumination on a monkish parchment.

I queue up to watch him. He makes me a group
Of solemn connoisseurs trying to see the brushstrokes.
I want to thumb the air in their knowing way.
I murmur *Chinese black*, I murmur *alizarin*.

But the little picture with four flirts and a delicate
Up-swinging's landed on another boulder.
He gives me a stained-glass look and keeps
Chick-chacking at me. I suppose he's swearing.

You'd expect something like oboes or piccolos
(Though other birds, too, have pebbles in their throats —
And of them I love best the airy skylark
Twittering like marbles squeezed in your fist).

Cul Beg looks away — his show's been stolen.
And the up-staged loch would yawn if it could.
Only the benign sun in his fatherly way
Beams on his bright child throwing a tantrum.

KINGFISHER

That kingfisher jewelling upstream
seems to leave a streak of itself behind it
in the bright air. The trees
are all the better for its passing.

It's not a mineral eater, though it looks it:
It doesn't nip nicks out of the edges
of rainbows. — It dives
into the burly water, then, perched
on a Japanese bough, gulps
into its own incandescence
a wisp of minnow, a warrior stickleback.
— Or it vanishes into its burrow, resplendent
Samurai, returning home
to his stinking slum.

GODDESS OF LUST

Her coif, her coiffure,
Her watch-chain ankles
Make dizzy the air
In igloos and Insurance Offices.
Airports remember her,
Cafés wear her scent.

She saunters with mirrors
Through holy congregations —
She's everywhere: except
She has always just left
The million sad rooms
Where love lies weeping.

That creepycrawly traversing the stone
six inches from my nose makes me a caveman
fanned by pterodactyls and roared at
by dinosaurs.

A butterfly dangles by, delicate
as a carrot leaf. If only it could write
its flowery memoirs. If only it could paint
the rich halls it has visited.

The weather doodles a faint cloud
on the blue
then pensively washes it out,
making the blue boastful.

There's something whirring
in the cat's mouth. It opens it
and a beetle flies out. The cat
is Amazement, in fur.

Hens sloven. But the cock
struts by — one can almost see
the tiny set of bagpipes
he's sure he's playing.

The sun's the same — pipemajoring
across space, where the invisible judges
sit, wrapped in their knowledge,
taking terrible notes.

PRESENTS

I give you an emptiness,
I give you a plenitude.
Unwrap them carefully —
one's as fragile as the other —
and when you thank me
I'll pretend not to notice the doubt in your voice
when you say they're just what you wanted.

Put them on the table by your bed.
When you wake in the morning
they'll have gone through the door of sleep
into your head. Wherever you go
they'll go with you and
wherever you are you'll wonder,
smiling, about the fullness
you can't add to and the emptiness
that you can fill.

THE SHIFTS OF SPRING

The gean tree invisibly unwrinkles its leaves.
A fox lies among hundreds of green croziers
that will uncoil and be bracken. From between two stones
in the Bay of Stinking Fish an otter protrudes
its World War One face, before bonelessly slipping
into the seamless water.

My mind is full of shifting planes
like cards in a conjuror's hands. They make
fans and concertinas and cascades
and sudden stills —
the ace of hearts: the five of clubs.
Am I changing in this weather
of transformation? I feel I'm a string
of trick shots in a film that's being made
without a camera.

I think of stolid summer
lying for miles on its fat haunches, hardly bothering
to reach up and pull down a cloud:
or winter, walking in its bones and greeting you
round any corner with its silly giggle:
or autumn, beautifully moping, pregnantly
self-obsessed.

But the cards slither and I'm staring at
the joker of spring. I steady myself. I take a straight look. . .
The fox has gone. But the gean tree's still working away
and the Old Bill otter's now peering across No-man's-land
from a dug-out camouflaged
with bladderwrack and blue bursts
of mussels.

HEROES

The heroes of legend
and the heroes of history
met, by looking
in a mirror.

And the heroes of legend
capered with joy,
crying,
'We're real, we're real!'

And the heroes of history
wept with rage
and wanted
to smash the mirror.

But that would mean they'd cease
to exist. So they dried their eyes
and assumed once more
their insufferable poses.

PRAISE OF A COLLIE

She was a small dog, neat and fluid —
Even her conversation was tiny:
She greeted you with *bow*, never *bow-wow*.

Her sons stood monumentally over her
But did what she told them. Each grew grizzled
Till it seemed he was his own mother's grandfather.

Once, gathering sheep on a showery day,
I remarked how dry she was. Pollóchan said, 'Ah,
It would take a very accurate drop to hit Lassie.'

And her tact — and tactics! When the sheep bolted
In an unforeseen direction, over the skyline
Came — who but Lassie, and not even panting.

She sailed in the dinghy like a proper sea-dog.
Where's a burn? — she's first on the other side.
She flowed through fences like a piece of black wind.

But suddenly she was old and sick and crippled. . .
I grieved for Pollóchan when he took her a stroll
And put his gun to the back of her head.

PRAISE OF A BOAT

The Bateau Ivre and the *Marie Celeste*,
The *Flying Dutchman* hurdling latitudes —
You could make a list (sad ones like the *Lusitania*
And braved puffed-up ones like the *Mayflower*).

Mine's called *the boat*. It's a quiet, anonymous one
That needs my two arms to drag it through the water.
It takes me huge distances of a few miles
From its lair in Loch Roe to fishy Soya.

It prances on the spot in its watery stable.
It butts the running tide with a bull's head.
It skims downwind, planing like a shearwater.
In crossrips it's awkward as a piano.

And what a coffin it is for haddocks
And bomb-shaped lythe and tigerish mackerel —
Though it once met a basking shark with a bump
And sailed for a while looking over its shoulder.

When salmon are about it goes glib in the dark,
Whispering a net out over the sternsheets —
How it crabs the tide-rush, the cunning thing,
While arms plunge down for the wrestling silver.

Boat of no dreams, you open spaces
The mind can't think of till it's in them,
Where the world is easy and dangerous and
Who can distinguish saints and sinners?

Sometimes that space reaches out
Till I'm enclosed in it in stony Edinburgh
And I hear you like a barrel thumping on head waves
Or in still water chuckling like a baby.

You've taken your stand
between Christy MacLeod's house
and the farthest planet.

The ideal shape of a circle
means nothing to you: you're all
armpits and elbows
and scraggy fingers that hold so delicately
a few lucid roses. You are
an encyclopedia of angles.

At night you trap stars, and the moon
fills you with distances.
I arrange myself to put
one rose in the belt of Orion.

When the salt gales drag through you
you whip them with flowers
and I think —
Exclamations for you, little rose bush,
and forty fanfares.

PRAISE OF A ROAD

You won't let me forget you. You keep nudging me
With your hairpin bends or, without a *Next, please,*
Magic-lanterning another prodigious view
In my skull where I sit in the dark with my brains.

You turn up your nose above Loch Hope,
That effete low-lier where men sit comfy
In boats, casting for seatrout, and whisper
Up the hill, round the crag — there are the Crocachs.

You're an acrobat with a bulrushy spine,
Looping in air, turning to look at yourself
And faultlessly skidding on your own stones
Round improbable corners and arriving safe.

When the Crocachs have given me mist and trout
And clogs of peat, how I greet you and whirl
Down your half-scree zigzags, tumbling like a peewit
Through trembling evenings down to Loch Eriboll.

MISS BOTTICELLI 1976

You'd never come ashore, cool Aphrodite,
on the frothy knuckles of waves. If you stood,
lasciviously still, on the most perfect scallop shell,
it would turn and dwindle you away.
For you're no landward lassie. You're the white enigma
of faking distances. Smoothly you wheel and turn
on meandering sea surfaces, still figure
of marble mists.

Yet across the bleakest maze
of a city bar, of a slip-slop café,
I suddenly see you looking at me
with a look I should drown in.
My glass wobbles down on the table
like a landing helicopter. I take your hand
and you teach me beautiful things
about garbage cans and supermarkets
and the Poseidon policeman standing
where four currents meet.

SMALL RAIN

The rain — it was a little rain — walked through the wood
                              (a little wood)
Leaving behind unexpected decorations and delicacies
On the fox by the dyke, that was eating a salmon's head.
(The poacher who had covered it with bracken wasn't going
                              to be pleased.)

The rain whisperingly went on, past the cliff all Picasso'd
With profiles, blackening the Stoer peat stacks, silvering
Forty sheep's backs, half smudging out a buzzard.
It reached us. It passed us, totally unimpressed.

Not me. I looked at you, all cobwebby with seeds of water,
Changed from Summer to Spring. I had absolutely no way of
                              saying
How vivid can be unemphatic, how bright can be brighter
Than brightness. You knew, though. You were smiling, and
                              no wonder.

FULFILLED AMBITION

With too much leg and not enough wing
the daddylonglegs helicopters
about the room,
outer space to him, where the lamp
blazes like Saturn.

A while ago,
this stumbling brown fragility
was a monster guzzling in the potato patch.

Then he was full of purpose
(without knowing it).
How he munched and munched — and all to become
that endearing eccentric now hanging
by one toe from the ceiling.

I nurse him outside and toss him
into a night full of planets.

A SIGH FOR SIMPLICITY

I like *so* and *therefore*: I like extensions.
It's one of my faults and a reason I'm afraid.
If only I could leave (where it's sunny and shady)
The physics of light to men of different passions.

If only I could see a hazelnut without thinking
Of monkish skullcaps. Does the fishing boat at the pier
Really rock like a bear? Is a mussel really *bearded*?
It's time I put the lady moon on my blacklist.

I groan, and think, If only I were Adam
To whom everything was exactly its own name —
Until one day the other appeared, the shameless
Demander of similes, the destroyer of Eden.

SEE WHAT YOU'VE DONE

I say comfortably
The core of the apple was sweet
and to hell with Eden
as I sway on my camel's back
through the eye
of that famous needle.

WATER

So that water might be
elephantine and pinpoint,
what an industry of air,
what transformations of heat.
And water goes off — it skulks
through the cracks in rocks,
jemmying them open:
or advances on parade, covering counties
with banners and bannerets. It trickles
nursery rhymes. It stuns a landscape
with its soft piledriver. It woos
planks ashore and liltingly
draws ships down
through its diminishing light.
A tree is its image, a bud
its cold candle flame, its amethyst,
its baby Lucifer and star of the morning.
The wastrel sun huffs off, but its light
is stored in ponds and lakes —
they beam in the dark, rustling
with the gentlest of frictions.

What mindlessness
in the buffeting of tides:
what revelation in a drizzling spray
with a round rainbow in it:
what lucidity
in the glass a woman hands
to a man.

LUCIFER FALLING

The black radiance
was Lucifer falling.
Space grieved for him
shuddering at its own guilt
and moons were never the same
after passing through
the gauze of his wings.
The crystal battlements shook
to hear him laughing;
and somewhere amid
the angelic jubilations
there was a small weeping,
forecast
of the earth to come.

MEANS TEST

I'd heard of a stony look. Was that one
You turned on me? Was I to be petrified?
But it seemed to me as beautiful as ever
And I walked from the house whistling into a sunset.

I took the look home and became uneasy.
I couldn't see it as other than limpid and shining.
Are you water? or diamond? I prefer things shifting
And lucid, not locked in a hard design.

I mustn't look at you with wrong eyes,
Inventing what I want to see. Turn to me now
And let me know if I'm a millionaire
Of water or a pauper of diamonds.

IMPOSSIBLE PRAYER

If I fold this paper smaller
and smaller and smaller till
it's an astronomer's Black Hole,
there's no saying what tanks and wallflowers
would rush into it:
there's no saying
what juicy conductors would drop their batons,
stunned by a silence in Mozart
or what sharks would open a school
for blue tits in the fields of barley:
who could guess what sad women
would file by there, to the sound
of banjos and rainy forests
or count the wounds redly flying in,
stickily weeping?

But I'm an unfolder.
I smooth the paper out, I press it
larger and larger
and stare dumbfounded
at what try to crowd on to it —
I beat them off, I wave them away.
I pray to some God or other
to give me back
that small smoothness,
that small whiteness.

SMALL LOCHS

He's obsessed with clocks, she with politics,
He with motor cars, she with amber and jet.
There's something to be obsessed with for all of us.
Mine is lochs, the smaller the better.

I look at the big ones — Loch Ness, Loch Lomond,
Loch Shin, Loch Tay — and I bow respectfully,
But they're too grand to be invited home.
How could I treat them in the way they'd expect?

But the Dog Loch runs in eights when I go walking.
The Cat Loch purrs on the windowsill. I wade
Along Princes Street through Loch na Barrack.
In smoky bars I tell them like beads.

And don't think it's just the big ones that are lordlily named.
I met one once and when I asked what she was called
The little thing said (without blushing, mind you)
The Loch of the Corrie of the Green Waterfalls.

I know they're just H_2O in a hollow.
Yet not much time passes without me thinking of them
Dandling lilies and talking sleepily
And standing huge mountains on their watery heads.

REPORT

All the time water is steeplejacking
up the insides of flowerstems.
All the time stones buried in a field
float up to the surface.
All the time the lordliest mountain
goes on becoming a plain where houses will send
friendly smoke over the bellowing of cattle.

And a woman pours milk from a jug,.
a doorhandle turns to let in happiness
and a doll spreadeagled on the floor says
I am the resurrection and the life.

And all the time
eyes change what they look at,
ears never stop making their multiple translations
and the right hand doesn't know, because it doesn't want to,
what the left hand is doing.

DISCOURAGING

Where anyway are answers? I think of that Greek
Drawing geometries in the sand. He thought he'd found some
Crouched like angelic toads in obtuse and acute angles
Or tangentially soaring off to touch other circles.
Happy fellow! He had more than one ground
For believing that find is a fruit of seek.

Walking in the umbrageous policies of my mind
I keep stepping in mantraps. (I'm only the tenant.
If ever I meet the owner I'll have some questions
To ask him.) The localest of explorations —
And I'm miraged, mosquitoed, shipwrecked, headhunted,
Boiled in a pot — something anyway unkind.

To question a microbe is to quizz
The supersuper universe. There seems no border
At all between things (except answer and question).
Poor Archimedes! He thought he was getting
Somewhere, when that soldier came by and a sword
Asked another question and cut short his.

The flower — it didn't know it —
was called dwarf cornel.
I found this out by enquiring.

Now I remember the name
but have forgotten the flower.

— The curse of literacy.

And the greed for knowing. —
I'll have to contour again
from the Loch of the Red Corrie
to the Loch of the Green Corrie
to find what doesn't know its name,
to find what doesn't even know
it's a flower.

Since I believe in correspondences
I shrink in my many weathers
from whoever is contouring immeasurable space
to find what I am like — this forgotten thing
he once gave a name to.

SUMMER EVENING IN ASSYNT

The green of Elphin
in this particular light
is its particular green.
It might be worn
by a royal, pale girl
in a Celtic legend.

I look up
at the eagle idling over
from Kylesku.
I look away
at the shattering waterblink
of Loch Cama.

I look down at my feet
and there's a frog
so green, so beautiful
it might be waiting in a Celtic legend
for the brave prince to come,
for the spell to go backward.

Hawks could teach bullets a thing or two —
see one precisely repeating
the terrified unpredictable zigzags
of a mountain pipit.

And gannets and aeroplanes — can a plane
turn over and backwards and
slam stunningly into the sea — to re-emerge
with a ruffle and begin unwinding
the same long spool of flight?

These are swift and beautiful. But watch
the gull, the slow flier, the airy loiterer
than can pause, dead still,
curved on the air
like a hand on a breast.